GW00361477

First printing, 2020.

1 2 3 4 5 6 7 8 9 10

Published in Canada by The Whamdoozer Company
Box 6636, Fort St. John, BC, Canada, V1J 4J1

ISBN 978-1-7772251-0-0

hookersandblowbooks.com

Hookers and Blow

SAVE CHRISTMAS

Written & Illustrated by Munty C. Pepin

"We need all of those presents
for the big party today."
"No problem!" said Hookers.
"We can help right away."

The snow was quite deep
and covered the road.
Blow got to work blowing
and could handle the load.

They travelled down Main Street
and straight out of town.
Drove up on Mount Dexter
then all the way down.

Just 'round the bend
Tom Transport soon did appear,
all covered in snow,
right up to his mirrors.

Blow cleared away the snow,
it didn't take long.
Now Hookers could check
what might have gone wrong.

Across bridges and train tracks,
Blow leading the way.
Up and down old Mount Dexter,
they soon made up the delay.

Lightning Source UK Ltd.
Milton Keynes UK
UKRC031405251021
392807UK00001B/6